This book belongs to

....

Copyright © 2021

make believe ideas ltd

The Wilderness, Berkhamsted, Hertfordshire, HP4 2AZ, UK.
6th Floor, South Bank House, Barrow Street, Dublin 4, D04 TR29, Ireland.

www.makebelieveideas.co.uk

Photographs courtesy of Shutterstock unless noted as follows:
Make Believe Ideas: 14bm, 15bm (fruit and vegetables), 20br (flower).

Bees do more than buzz

by Lucy Waterhouse

make
believe
ideas

Get the most from this reader

Before reading:

- Ask questions such as, "Can you see the beehives in this picture?"

- Discuss what your child thinks will happen in the book and why. Check after reading to see if this prediction was correct.

- Relate the topic to your child's world. For example, say: "Where have you seen bees in our garden?"

During reading:

- Prompt your child to sound out unknown words. Draw attention to neglected middle or end sounds.

- If your child makes a mistake, ask if the text makes sense and allow him or her time to correct it before helping.

- Occasionally, ask what might happen next, and then check together as you read on.

- Monitor your child's understanding. Repeated readings can improve fluency and comprehension.

- Keep reading sessions short and enjoyable. Stop if your child becomes tired or frustrated.

■ ■

After reading:

- Discuss the book. Encourage your child to form opinions with questions such as, "Did you like the ending? Why or why not?"

- Help your child work through the fun activities at the back of the book. Then ask him or her to reread the story. Praise any improvement.

At the park, Tom jumped behind his sister. "Why are you hiding?" asked Kate. "The bees! I'm scared they might sting me," said Tom.

8

"They'll only sting you if you hurt them," Kate said. "How much do you know about bees? Bees are our friends. Let me show you how useful they are."

When you see a bee on a flower, it is doing an important job. The bees are carrying pollen from one flower to another.

10

Look! I can see yellow
pollen on this bee's legs.

11

Plants need pollen to make seeds.
The seeds grow into new plants.
Without bees, some of these plants would
die out. Bees are very helpful insects.

12

13

Much of our food comes from plants, such as fruit and vegetables. If bees were not around to carry pollen, there would be fewer plants. Without bees, we would have less food to eat.

This beekeeper thinks bees are useful, too. Many bees make honey, and she is collecting some of the honey from the bees.

Here is the honey the bees made in their hive. Without bees, we would have no honey.

Bees aren't as bad as you think. They work very hard. We need to take care of the bees because they take care of us.

19

Bees might be small, but they have an important job. I wonder if other people know how much bees help us? I'm going to tell everyone how useful they are.

How Bees Help Us

Bees help plants make seeds.

Discussion Questions

1 Where is the pollen on the bee's body?

2 How do we get honey?

3 Do you think bees are important? Why?

✏ Sight Words ✏

Learning sight words helps you
read fluently. Practise these
sight words from the book.
Use them in sentences of your own.

might

would

from

see

some

much

how

these

❧ Rhyming Words ❧

Can you find the rhyming pairs?
Say them aloud.

bees

knees

food

ring

sting

store

more

rude

Read the words, and then trace them with your finger.

jump

flower

important

pollen

yellow

vegetable

beekeeper

collect

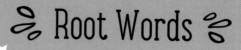

Root Words

Match each word with
its root word.

Root words:

jump

sting

use

carry

grow

less

Words:

useful

carried

growth

jumped

unless

stinging

Words for Comparing

Follow the lines to match each word with its comparison and superlative.

great

small

smaller

hard

bad

greater

worse

greatest

harder

smallest

worst

hardest